THE
BUTTERFLY GATE
-POEMS & PROSE-

Nefisa UK
Brighton – Washington DC

The Butterfly Gate

Copyright © Y. Misdaq 2011

All rights reserved. This book, or parts thereof, may not be reprinted or distributed in any form without prior permission of the author. However, those wishing to cite, discuss or use this book in any way beneficial to humankind are encouraged to contact the author.

03. Pret coffee & sandwich

Published by Nefisa UK
NEFI-BK04
First Edition

ISBN 10: 0-9555024-3-8
ISBN 13: 978-0-9555024-3-9

Preface (to be read at the end)

I must apologize for 'the poem of delicious affirmation'. Other than that first sentence, you should not read the rest of this preface until after finishing the book. *Really*, skip it. As long as you know I have apologized sincerely for it, you can now move on and read what's important, the poems. I will place a marker for you ♥ ; return to your heart later… I also apologize for not addressing any other themes from the rest of this book, but this poem is rather important. I am now over three years removed from having written the aforementioned poem, and have, since the very moment I wrote it, wrestled with whether or not to include it in this book. I tried all kinds of ways of getting around it, but ultimately, it is part of the story. More importantly, I hope it is relatable to others in a shared context, insomuch as we all are 'modern' humans undergoing a shared experience, trying to make our affirmations, trying to make sense of this life we find ourselves in. Struggle is inevitably involved; discord struck.

A great deal of contemporary Western art falls short for me because of its ultimate inability to get past this concept of discord, or rather, because of its romantic celebration of discord as some sort of ultimate truth. This idea that discord / chaos is 'the only real truth' and so on. Any intelligent and observant human living in the present world and not looking inwards enough will probably arrive at that same conclusion. And although I believed the idea (particularly as it was expressed in 'arthouse' films and, in some way, *all* of the contemporary arts) to be *spiritintellectually* unrefined and frankly passé many years before writing the poem, I realize now that I had, nonetheless, bought into it fully on some less perceptible, purely emotional level. I had begun to see little rhyme or reason. Struggle with something you are not big enough to face inevitably does this to you; intellectually you may understand a thing to be false, but emotionally you will still be enslaved to it. It's the same reason teenagers (and all too many adults) repeatedly get back together with that same boyfriend/girlfriend, even though they know they are terrible for each other. Thus is the poem of delicious affirmation. I leave it in the final draft unedited in the hope that for any other young humans who may feel as passionate and confused as I did, it will offer a strange energy, a temporary liberation from this preposterous life of narrow number-knowledge, just as it did for me when I wrote it. Chained and yet wanting to butterfly away on wind.

This book begins with serene, pure moments from my hometown of Brighton (pgs 1-10) before I moved across the ocean. Needless to say those serene moments were well and truly gone once I moved here, to this mad mushed-up mirage of a magic wonderland. What stays once you physically leave a place? Nothing from that place. The particular serenity of one place will not follow you to another. You bring only what is in your heart. And traveling helps you sort out the one from the other, separating ones environment and all its hand-me-downs from ones own soul, innate personality; *nature*. And so, from the moment I arrived, The Butterfly Gate became a receptacle for something quite different than what it had been when I started it so peacefully in Brighton. It became a book of what I thought were *euphoric* poems!

Well, some of them are. But they are of a type that is euphoric through desperation. As the afterword of the next book will more accurately inform you, I was in a strange country where I knew nobody and had no limits (see *Spilling Kingdoms*) and when it wasn't miserable, it was often incredibly exciting. This book is about the soul trying to break free, without any guidelines on how to do so. And although at the time, I would not only have shunned, but perhaps even spat on, the idea of 'guidelines,' (especially concerning the soul!) I came to realize later that Absolute Freedom, as a state of being, noble concept, aspiration, does not come about via absolute freedom in ones actions. Such 'freedom' enacted without adequate discipline, the occasional sacrifice and, yes, *restriction* leads to burn-out; burn-out leads to unhappiness; unhappiness leads to darth vader. I was young, and I did not know. 2008's 'affirmation' was extreme laughter and deep sadness laying side-by-side, inexplicably linked in some current of intense desire and wanting. Spiritual and totally sensual. It was a hatred of the material world, laying side by side with a wish to succeed in it, to conquer it completely. To run far away from the rat-race, and to *have* everything.

Ultimately (and the poems themselves began to realize this) the excitements and desires I felt could not satiate or sustain me. Indeed, the excitements I felt being a stranger in a new land had come as a result of seeing myself as an actor in a really funny and good film – something tempting for all of us to think at times when our lives take seemingly 'surreal' turns. But as wondrous as they may sometimes be, <u>our lives are not films</u>. And such thoughts only betray the fact that we often employ / pimp our 'new experiences' making them act as selfish, ego-boosting shields, medals of honour, and ultimately barriers to Real experience. I keep saying we, I mean me. Beyond the self lies Universes. And looking to ones own excitement and ones own pleasure, as derived from ones own life-experiences, is not always the best key towards exploring Universes of Eternity. And if you say to me now that *you don't want to explore eternity*, I will say listen to your own childhood; it will prove you wrong. <u>We are adventurers</u>; it is only this world that has made us 'adults' – too scared to admit that amazing, exciting fact.

Slowly, at the time this book of statements and assertions was concluding, huge questions had begun forming under the surface. The poems were not yet fully conscious of them, blinded as they were by the surety of strongly felt passions and the excitement of temporal things not having completely worn off, however with the following book (see *Spilling Kingdoms*) they would start asking for expression, and later on (see *Palace Prayers*) to demand expression, ultimately demanding of their author a completely new direction and orientation. Excitements are all fueling; and they all soon begin to empty out. The engine begins to demand a higher grade of fuel when once the soul begins to feel the immense call of the ethereal, the transcendental, the Beautiful. You can't go home again; the only way is Up.

So he looked down from the comfortable, sensible chessboard he had been dancing upon. Looked down at the Stars, at the Sea of Mysticism; began to think about jumping.

Yusuf Misdaq,
July 1st 2011
Brooklyn, New York

The Butterfly Gate

First Boy, Butterfly Born

Here I am
Sat, stone

A diamond-stud
Pinned into the soft-grass

The balance-waves of flux-life
Are stasis-like
All pushing and pulling with equality
.Not lonely.

The lovely winds
Fold aloft above
For their own happiness

Falling a little on me
As after-thought

It's in this position
With the sun on my hair
That my egg is cracked
And majesty evaporates
Seeping sleepily with lulled pleasure
Across the waiting town

A Deep Feeling of Bliss

The feeling is accompanied by a
Delicate flutter in the stummy[1]
As if you are nervous
At the prospect of goodness occurring

The body is somehow unpeaceful
Through many veils
There is a dulled jitteriness

Is it the squeezing
Of the soul
As it tries to sneak out of the body?

Creep out without me knowing
In the late afternoon?

---

[1] stomach

<u>Remember to look up to the big big sky</u>

Endless possibility which is constantly in motion

And at night time when it twinkles

Everything open and waiting

Inviting you to take a step

Step in
Out there

The earth will shake once you've begun to touch it.

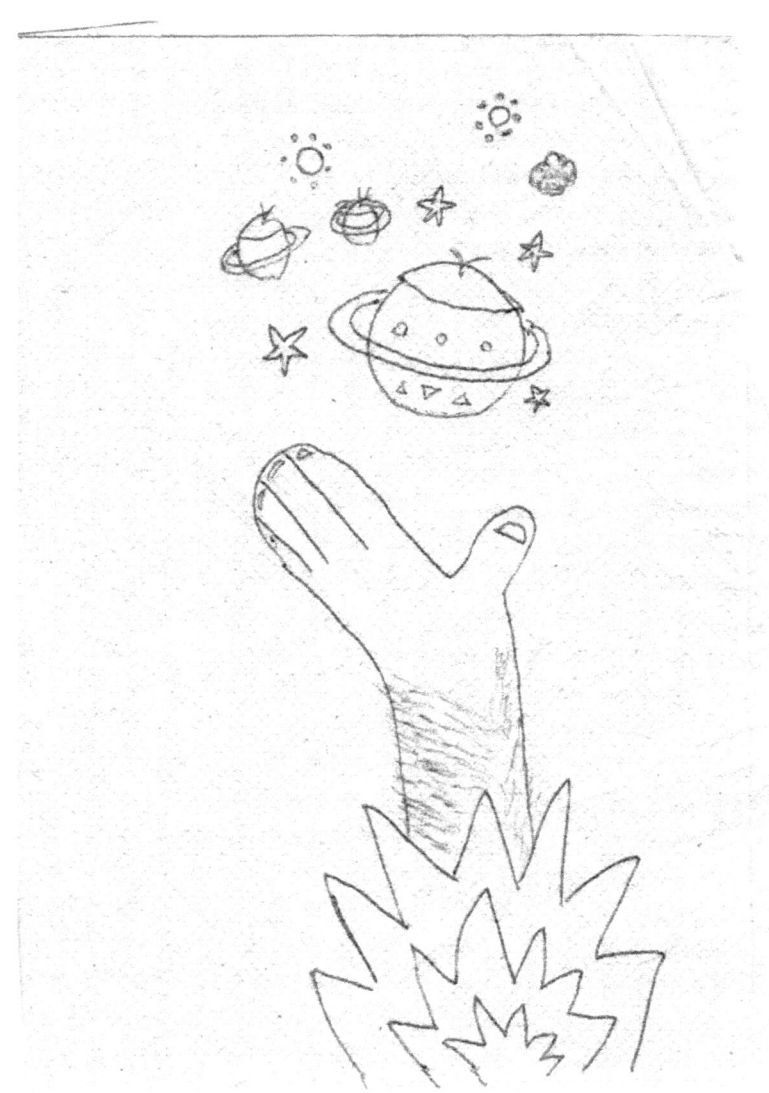

Change returns success… Action brings good fortune – Syd Barrett

Meem

.Sea of iron.

.Solid Body.

      God of Pharaoh
          God of Millionaires
              God of Bush
                  God of Me.

.Gold God.   .God of Gold.

Endless Runner
Surface-sweeping a billion miles on the belly at
Beautiful, clarified speed.

Flatline Palaces with drifting dunes and
Scattered puff-mountains for gardens
One thousand seeable miles away from your evolution-
window

    Where each look,
    Love and
    Late-coming thought is
    Lonely for no sun and
    Fearful for no shadow

    In the endless afternoon

Springday

Delicate day, 11 o'clock
Sun living in peace with my skin

Spring. Easter Holiday
No time limits, no deadlines

I awake early, even though I don't have to
And the day seems expansive, open and long

Inside my heart there is a gentle clock that ticks only forwards. It doesn't know how much time remains; it only dreams how much is yet to come. Forwards it moves, not so much ticking as surging, silently, in peace it swims gently. And you hear the folding water, calmly rippling and the droplets trickling.

Soon a fact, a face or a facet of something will stir me back into the mixture of Earth. I shall be diluted down amidst the swirls of problem and pasture. But again and again my soul pushes for its place at the new peak, where in purity it settles and its true colours become.

Now I hear a drill. It's time for housework.

Idea

My mind es mi mundo. Solipsism.

The brain floats in the skull
Floats in fluid.
That's a fact.
There is no pressure on it.
It's not in a cage.
It is free.

The lack of pressure
The fact that it floats
Probably gives a good indication as to why it is capable of such magnificence.

I would like, therefore, to have my entire body float.

I will look into that.

"Possibility" / On Primrose Hill

Wafts of word-wind
  Shimmer through and reach me

The shaking wind and the word 'possibility'
Which is –struck like a bell– spoken
Small and immaculately crafted in a rich metal
It resonates and twinkles
Like a French or Italian word.

Its dark shadow is 'Portentous'

Its aspiration is a positive one
An aspirant, soaring, or
Waiting to be released from its syllable-cage
So that it may soar

Once it has become its aspiration.

<u>Elmhurst, Queens</u>

Beyond a double-paned wall of glass and
Bin liners and a
Rusted metal fence

There is a green tree wavering tenderly in the *while*[2]

The fresh, worth, while

---

[2] Wind

<u>Music</u>

        High

    There in a warm recess

Draw out some resonant cascades
Pine them out

Waterfall them down onto a wooden bass timbre
Which takes shape in a triangle pattern

When once that has established itself alone
–As a reassuring and experienced presence–

Let a *mi*nute-flute fly one glissando
To conquer a small Kingdom
A majestic little mound of green grass
Curving without calibration
Round as sound and happy

The flutes tone is warm and deeper
As though its sound rose from inner the human chest
Blown not by air, but rather
Fill'd and stream'd with warm, weightless milk

Why wait
Why watch

          wondering
We're
          wandering

Wash with loosely spilling water jet-streams
A drunken circular cymbal of ancient times with

        Trophy'd
                Trustful
                        Rustic timbre

No rhythms of a fretted, frozen nature
Rather, the age-old cymbal hiss or
Huss (for it is a broad and deep cymbal)
Trickles freely in sunny circles
Like an bumbling happy old woman called Daisy
Watering sunflowers with a
Watering can

Trickles

Like a child approaching the age where he should
Know better
              But does not yet
Urinating in his front garden with trousers
Pulled down around his ankles
Laughing unlimited with red cheeks and curly light hair

Let it rain!
Let it rain under the childhood sun.

This song may go nowhere
Say no thing
And continue tinkering around
Without any jaw-dropping solo

Or anymore fresh ingredients
And it would still be beautiful
For all time

think he won't?

Douh Douh Douh Douh

The heartiest feign.
Surl-in-fe-jonah whaleington.
Laffid-eye drops-a-moisture.
Fe-terliffer, jonz-an-oyster.
Sa-foanika, lamulet pediment.
Lamulet
Lamulet
Lamulet.

There in my bar of soap
     At the center
   Is the heart of me

There in the solid hand grasped bar
Of all places
         Would you believe it
   My protected heart

A vision - A ribbon - A rhythm

Melting like chocolate into history

Horizon life

Where there lies a horizon, and on it a leaving light
There, on that positive wave is where you must place your life

Wherever things slowly drag and fade away
That's where to invest.

Let these days fall off your shoulders and let them leave.
Let them roll off you like shower droplets
When your eye is on the sun from the window
Let the showers wash over you

With each polishing moment of break and sobriety
Each soliloquy
Each delicately phrased thought and
Each forgotten one too

We will be thrust into the great darkness
Where we shall remain until The Great Piecing

When that black cellar is illuminated

Regarding the Winter son, warmly
For D.S. & Mika Yamagata

Sun tinted lullaby

Oh, the window sill got warm when the
Parent put her hand on it

Walking into the warm silent room
Thick, soft, socks
                Clean, shining wooden floor

Staring at her son, asleep by the window
Handsome face and clean hair with the
Sleeping smile of a perfect child

All that she knew - felt from life

Now looking at him as son

Her beautiful son

Give it to me (recited to imaginary hip-hop beat)

I'm a mind-rusty
  But trust me, I'll
Never fake dust or
Pretend that I'm rustic
Trust it

Nails as young and old
As my serious developing Soul

Soul is strong like a smiling father
Soul is something soft but harder
Whites of ocean
Black around stars

Dreams remembered that's so close but far

Faces so afraid of the final flight, four
Eyes unfocused in a leap of love

<u>Lick</u> the days to come
<u>Spit</u> the shit that's done

    Let the future come

    Let the engine hum

    Let the engine run

Manifestover the Moon

Selling off 1st Editions of my latest fresh skin to the
Gullible Lovers of Earth who want not, but for a
Single touch of sincerity
And that, that I will give them

With bleeding pleasure
        My goods and my clots
In all their drippingness
All their fathomless atomness

Who but me shall fall upon my sword?
Who but me shall melt their reward?
With dirt rising all around, who but all of us shall
Take out spoons and shovels and
Slide out the invading forces?

The faux-bohemians
The flaccid dignitaries
Who seek to lull us under their control
To take us by sleep
By their slow calculated approach to 'the dilemma'
To brand us as we dream
Whereupon we awaken as slaves
To an alarm clock
     A tie
       A commute
          And a false laugh for

       Foolish ambition

Still sleeping
> we are !

And thank God for that !

Now

These twinkling nights are like daydreams as I sleep and scheme to pull out my pockets and release the goblins and dustbins and paraffin. If I don't let the world have some of my insides then how boring would the world be? I must induce this happy vomit. So must you. must must.

Set it on fire and reject it.

If we all danced like criminals and insane people then one day we might taste the salty air of the sea, we might be on one of earths edges feeling free. If we all forgot who we were.

And somewhere under the moonlight of the timeless night somebody played 'Stand By Me' by Ben E. King on crackly speakers over an old wooden boardwalk by a warm beach. The romantic strings of innocence and experience. The religious words of love. And a child like me walked past with family and remembered the moment for the rest of his adult life; and a couple stood inside one another, leant on some gate and inhaled the same style of love, they felt the moments tide reach up to their necks and drown them; and a lonely young man nearby was all destroyed and burnt inside as he cursed the earth; and insects moved around them all, keeping everything constant and continuous and connected.

Fertile Miles / Alone, Continue Artist!

Fertile.
I've funded fertile miles
And defaulted payments on wasted zero space
Throughout the journey so far

I've thanked nobody
And received no help
Throughout the so-far soliloquy

And where are you now
That you've never been there to begin with?

All the flowers do is desire me
Give me ultimatums and try to own me

"I belong to this whole world," I say
Half-convinced of the loftiness and romance
One quarter convinced
As the cold winter breath runs away from me
Away from the dark alleyway in which I stand solitaire

An extended mile of grass-strip unfurls from my finger
And beckons the silly young artist forwards;
A way away from the black alleyway

Fertile mile.

'Magination. Beckoning.

Approach to Turquoise Dome

We are forwarding unto the Palace now
On horseback

Over the dunes booms the tip of turquoise dome that
Whispers like a blue flame

And when in full view
Even from a distance
It takes possession of our thought and vanity

Giant towering flame of *refinery finery*

'Come,'
       it says
As the hooves make soft pummels into the sand
As we face into its voluptuous dome

'Come to belong'

Everything Appeared Here

Can you imagine from one single idea
Everything appeared here
Understanding makes my truth crystal clear - Rza

The vast expanse of desert sand is seen from a panoramic view. You have the wide angled view of this large, warmed area, because you have let life pass you by through the years, rolling off you with ease. Those who clung to everything would never be allowed such a released, open view. You have the bigger picture in sight and as a result, see the sunlight happening. Rain happens on occasion also. This orange glow is yours to witness and keep as you please.

Twenty feet square, over there, in the middle of your view wanders a bison. It's through her that you see gravity being lost in the area. Her tonnes of meat and heart are lifted up, gently raised above the ground. She begins to drift in mid-air, her shadow drifting with her below, confirming everything. All around her is calm and silence. She is calm and silence, staring in your direction neither confused nor scared as she floats up high there.

It was years of a moment later that the exact amount of sand rose up in a perfectly flat square. It became level with her, existing in front of her eyes, and then it danced. The speed at which it danced and the styles with which it went rendered it impossible for you to ever describe to another human being again. So full stop.

The shape that this sand decided upon, some time when time had become irrelevant, was a small square area, resting just under the bison's feet. It then decided to grow into a larger square. This involved tonnes of further sand being lifted from the same area directly beneath the bison (although there was never an appearance of a loss of sand on the earth from which it came.) Everything was untouched. Soon it was a large flat square surface at least fifteen feet in each direction, and paper-thin. It was a floor in the air, which built itself around the bison, supporting her beautiful legs, her powerful body.

Around the edges of this floating floor, sprouting upwards towards the sky, as well as downwards toward the ground, swirls and patterns of sand began to grow, with the same indescribable style and speed at which the sand first began dancing. These were extensions of the sand from the floor, somehow appearing with unstoppable regularity. The swirls kept happening, and they were always odd in number; you believed they were odd in number. Some of the beautiful patterns that grew into existence made no sense to you whatsoever, they curled inside themselves impossibly, somehow warping and growing in ways that suggested laughter, giving you a feeling of power and euphoria. One danced like a rocket twirling around and around as it shot up into the sky like no bird could, thinning its consistency as it straightened itself out and faded away amidst the high blue. Others were of a more intense nature, silent sand, thick and heavy, unfurling in the time-span of a dream until, at some point in the past or present, you realised it was inches from your nose. The ends of it curled up creating a sand-sculpted index finger, which stood out of the solid mass of intense brown sand. That arm, that mass, was coloured like brown-sugar but the pieces were smaller, finer than any substance you had seen. The index finger shape just centimetres away from you buzzed in and out of existence with the wind, signifying one, in perfect form.

All it took was a step sideways away from this dominant, all-powerful structure and you could continue to witness the almost complete fortress of magnificence which floated some twenty feet above the ground, housing this bison of belief, which still blinked calmly as the final realities of sand were invading themselves into existence. Impossible though it was, each piece made perfect sense during and after construction. Continuous construction was beautiful, every one of them moved smoothly until they ended their patterns with such personality, such unique attributes. But when they ended they didn't end. They glinted and demanded interpretation. You thought all was completed when your weak eyes eventually detected the final strand working its way into life amidst the jungle of confirmed realities. This final strand was the smallest and quietest moving, curling again but on a smaller scale, intricate as calligraphy or an impossible ballet; its small movements were contrasted by the one thing that had characterised all of these varying strands: constancy. The strands never stopped until they were complete, they were revealed constantly and flowed perfectly like language and chemistry between people.

It's final curl, a surprisingly small one, left the image complete. One thing were you able to utter in staring at the final mercy, "The Most Subtle."

It was one word. It took you time of time to name them all, which you did quietly in your mind. You saw it that day and knew you could never explain it once it left. It was your experience to keep, always reminding you.

Years later you are, as you always were, uncurling, much slower and much more hesitantly than the sand of delight uncurled at that very real moment in time. Your way is flawed but attempting. Broken but aspiring.

Remember.

In an Avid Editing Suite

Welcome to Whatever It Becomes

Here the salivations run on into red carpets toward
    Thrones
Here the lust dissipates into dust
Here your ego is full'd up with love and
No longer hungry

Welcome to your delicious dreams

Where the harmonica sneezes in and out of prisons and
Homes

Dancing on its way to climax
Where the water envelops all and keeps you tall
Where you breathe in

Second Butterfly

A flight
Lite flite
Takes kite

Forget close-ups of brownies
With warm chocolate steaming from the centriheart

Forget dark wooden interiors
Warm condensation

Forget the word 'succulent' or 'wholesome'
Forget yeast, bonded bread in all its forms

Whatever a Clearwater Fish makes you feel like
Imagine that feeling

Up in the air

A Completely Uneventful Day (Fajjr's Reward)

Oh dear Lord, I am excited

Present on this marching day of rolling, thrilling news

A day which started with
Discipline and dawn
                    is concluding with
Deliverance and euphoria

I'm so thrilled to be a part of this world, to take place in the street scenes for fleeting moments and make smiling eye-contact with shaking old men and give my seat up for all flavours of wonderful women and hitch a ride on the piggy-back of any child at play.

I couldn't be happier to be swinging low under the
Day-time half-moon.
To be tripping across the arc
Eternally
Rainbow snowing
And skiing through the supple and willing air
Interceding and confronting
Every single atom

I don't know what the silent explosion of future holds in her secretive, gathering arms. I see only the vague reflections of light shimmering up onto her body. I can't imagine the taste either, but despite that, I keep on biting and licking the oxygen around me. As if this life were unreal and dreams made more sense.

Can't stop myself.

The Jiant Inside

I'm a donkey rubbing itself up against a warm radiator
Trying to be happy

I'm a fat man in love with hope as the sun rises

It's a new day. It's a new life

I'm a smile exploding all over the dead bystanders
Bringing them back to life

Massage yourself
Bring out your dandelion
    Cultivate your full potential

It's waiting for you

In your written tapestry
   (Which doesn't need you to believe in it)
There are buses leaving bus stops
Heading to Rajasthan's and Zanzibar's and
Newfoundland's and Godthab's and
Wellington's... Of the mind

Each bus hopes in its heart that you are on it
But if not there will be plenty more coming along

        Buses of Opportunity are
        Blood cells of Destiny

Dynamism of Man

Retina opens and what floods in?

I tell you it's a blue light
I tell you it's a soft yellow
I tell you tonight it's a moon as bright as the sun

And it makes music swirl and ghost. The music bounces off the walls of our heart chambers, burning itself up in energy and fizzing into blood which speeds like fast cars through our physical inches

The dynamism of man is this:

> I'm standing perfectly still and yet I feel as though the world belongs to me.

Falling Asleep

Sunken solitaire
Air noole
Shangrin-Stablehoff
Blurtle.
Skao-sens.
Toshikri.
Tantamount to borderline something-burgers.
Egyptian sunset, sea-smell
Heavy regret, bill-I-set.
Yarning. Pining. Toilet-silence.
Orange relationships. Sanguine.
Die like happiness.
Semi-conscious, gentle tickles of Tigris River.
.In the center.
Clarity. Concerts of colour in clarity.
Fuzz. Come over lere. Sere.
Go over pear. Lines love me. Inventing lines
Inside them, aliving them.
Lie in the logic of Lilly-cese.
Silent Pallycese.
Sanguinetti. Common sense was spaghetti.
I love imperfection.
Let it love for me.

Dearest Day-Digger:

Delight in finding ore and minerals
Densely packed inside the day

Deliver it whole unto the Lord and
Let the air of poets delineate

Let the swish of existence pick apart

With time
        With hands

The refined fragments
Delicate and sub-atomic
Which make for a holy hour

Praise-worthy
Passing

75 BPM from Victor Ramos

Oh my Lordness, Oh my Lordness!
As I sift through the winds of lawlessness.
As I sift and shy through the winds of lawlessness,

The snakes and ladders of social interaction leave me perpetually disappointed.

> and so here i have come
> inside music
> inside sound to close my eyes and picture it here.

A dark place. Yes, it's getting clearer now its outdoors, it looks a little like yoda's home, all foggy except it's blue everywhere, a warm blue and it's not as damp; there are trees everywhere.

> it's a blue forest at night time

And this
Thick midnight mist must make my mind magical.

I smile at the 3 midnight butterflies as they pass me like that fleeting feeling of love I felt back on earth once.. Running through me. Dark purple butterflies and they're glowing for each other; luminosity what a thing!

Before they go I ask, "what are you doing up so late?"

Two of them continue on as if I were talking to someone else or as if they were too happy to stop, but the other one looks back at me, flying still, fluttering its purple wings and radiating juiceous gaseousness in drops and vibrations.

It flies back to me, making a bold statement by letting its two friends continue on into the delightfully wicked night. This night that holds surprises and slow grins. The slow grin guilds across my face as butterfly number one comes towards me. Closer and closer and closer.,...Now it's resting on my nose. I look directly into it's eyes, directly into them. It's the first time I've felt equal to a butterfly before. And even though it's on my nose I'm aware that I'm not cross eyed; I am straight; both my eyes are one.

They see like the sun.
                        A totalitarian warmth vision.

I run towards the mustard field with crunching autumn leaves on my feet and the drifting smell of summer nights on the trees that rush past me.

Butterfly number one is on my nose still.

I see the huge moon reflecting on the wide open field. And I smell the wild smell. It's wild.

I am a beast of the absolute wilderness.

Oh my Lordness ! OH MY LORDNESS,
As I dance through the fibres of paradise-ness !

Commuting Underground
==

I'm a lucky boy to be sitting. What a packed train! How lucky! And I'm on the inside seat, so no one expects me to give up my seat! Tee-hee, I can get away with it! Hee-hee. And maybe I can get away with *other* things too, tee-hee! What a TREAT! Yes! It's like the toy you always wanted as a child suddenly APPEARING in your bedroom, right at the peak of your desire for it! Despite the fact that mum & dad wouldn't get it for you! Hee-hee!
There it is!

I'm safely sided into my black window seat by the giant thigh of a giant man who has a kind aura and wears ski-gear. I can tell the clothes he is wearing but in actuality I have not looked up at his face yet, and it's been five minutes!

Let me look.

   -Can I?

Well, who's stopping me?

   -No-one!

But I feel I should ask.

   -Why?

Because you shouldn't be free to do whatever you want... That's not fun. It's more nice to be granted it!

-But by whom? Just who are you asking, by jove!?

I think I'm asking God.

-And how would you expect to receive an answer?

I don't know.

-Richie Dawkins would see that as the main flaw in your thinking. Since you cannot be sure, what's the point? There's probably no God, he'd say, so relax and enjoy your life!

But I am enjoying it! BUT I AM!!

-But you cannot prove God exists! Doesn't that shame you beyond belief? Aren't you ashamed of your silly old-fashioned self? Don't you know what sarcastic and witty people like Christopher Hitchens would do to you if you ever locked horns with them on a discussion programme? Aren't you thoroughly ashamed?

Well. I can't say that I am, *hactually*![3] Know why?

-No, why?

Because I remember once not too long ago, when I wasn't sure if I could kiss a girl. The situation was absolutely

---

[3] Red Dwarf, series 01, episode 02

balanced. On the one hand, she had said a few things which made me think she might encourage me in it. But on the other hand, which was a bigger hand, I might have misconstrued her words entirely! Skewed them to mean precisely what I wanted them to mean! But there I was! Suddenly standing up and looking right down at her, for no good reason, with no words, beyond explanation! Staring at her in the dark with her looking back. And then, after a few seconds of never-always, know what I did?

-What? What!!?

I PLUNGED IN!

-Did you?

I DID!

-And what happened? Pray tell, dear sir, what happened???

I kissed her! Yes! And she LIKED IT! Do you hear me? SHE LLLLIKED IT! And before I knew what in the world was going on, we found ourselves involved in some strange face-dance of agreement and polishing. And I was cleaning her face like a cat. And I found myself saying all these WONDERFUL THINGS!

-Like what?

Like, "You're perfect," and, "I want to make you feel happy."

All whispers! Whispers and whiskers and vespers!

> -Wow! Wish something like that had happened to me at Oxford! Well anyway, I think I see your point. You are saying that being <u>unsure</u> does not equate directly to being <u>incorrect</u>.

Or even shameful! Or even ignorant! In fact, *unsure* can be one of the very highest stations a human can arrive at!

> -Yes…

Oh…

> -What?

Well, the man is leaving!

> -And? What did he look like?

Well… He did look tired. White, but with a red face. I suppose he *could* have been gentle. Gosh and he really was tall! A gentle giant! That'd be nice, wouldn't it?

> -Yes. Yes, everyone loves a gentle giant.

They do, don't they? It's like a noble failure.
Or a very cool old person.
Or a … a …

No I'm finished. Hehe.

God's people

Galaxy brown fades volume serene hum human motion calmly becoming and humming and strumming and singing and bringing it all to the moment, where? The moment in heart, the essence of heart, the tiger of expression, the courage of truth, which is wheat. The courage of wheat and the toil of the truth-tellers who nurture it, perfumed sweat spinning away from their wise, raising foreheads, from their long black hair, back into the brown earth of their brown skin. Their fertile bodies make birth earth and surf.

King & Tofting

A King stands at the edge of a mountain with thick heavy snow all in motion around him. It is five thousand years ago. The empire sky is grey, overcast in its entirety. It is not fully light. His white long beard remains still in the icy wind. His intelligent, narrowed eyes inspect the scene before him as if something were wrong, as if this wind and snow had an entirely different, foreboding meaning.

His servant, a round, hobbling hunchback who tends to his royal horse, comes up behind him and asks him, in his simple way, if everything is okay.

The King does not turn around. Staring out at the snowy plains and the vast sky in front of him, he says, "One day, Tofting, there shall be men of such low repute that they would live in small rooms, entirely alone, rarely seeing the light of day, bereft of tradition and of culture. They will be slaves unto a force known simply as.... INTER-NET."

Tofting scratched his head as if everything were normal, squinted his eyes to keep out the snow, which was blowing in his direction. Then, struck by the five second fools-delay, he suddenly looked puzzled, and repeated the alien word, "Interrr-net?"

"Yes Tofting. Inter-net." Said the King with his refined tone and confident voice of nobility, before carefully removing his cloak, which was made of fine, light metal. He first untied it from the right side and then the left, then, after folding it, draped it neatly over Tofting's waiting, outstretched hands. Tofting was dressed in a simple woollen jacket which was tied together with a piece of string and his bare knees were exposed to the elemental forces, which worked upon him incessantly, ensuring he would not live beyond 38 years (quite normal). The noble King, still facing forwards, then took his sword off his belt and held it in front of him, so that it lay before the magnificent view, a precursor.

The sun was suddenly seen, its delicate arc, glinting from the horizon, sharp and purely white.

"Those people will not know the sword, Tofting. They will be people of ease and luxury, luxury the likes of which you or I have never seen. They shall not know suffering, except that sort of suffering which one might feel when one loses a sheep or an ass. They shall eat, entertain themselves, and be merry. And they will know not the sword."

Tofting picked his nose and stared on, bewildered by the images his mind showed him.

"If I were to run myself through with this sword right now, Tofting, I should avoid the risk of being a forefather to one of these swines."

Tofting grew nervous. He wanted to tell his master not to do it, but he had learned from experience that the King's pauses in speech often heralded great surprises in the ensuing sentences.

"Alas, the seed has already been planted in mankind by our Maker. I am but one man and my demise would make little difference. I cannot stop that weak generation from appearing on our mother [planet]. I cannot stop the streets packed with sterile faces; people whose senses will be entirely cut off from the natural world, who will be too enraptured with *Eye-phone technologius* to even speak a word of cheer to their neighbour. There will be no Kings at that time, Tofting."

"What'll there be then, O lord? Tell us what there'll be!"

"There shall be money, Tofting. Invisble money, for women, money for popp'd corn and money for DaViD's. DaViD's of all regions. This money shall rule the world. Your ancestors shall be poor, and mine shall be like the rest. Comfortable; laughing at puerile jokes and imitating others, with no desire to be anything other than accepted. This is our future Tofting. Our future of transience."

Tofting picked his nose again and stared down at the floor. He did not know what transience meant.

"There is only one thing that we are capable of doing to remedy the situation, Tofting. And even that is not entirely within the spheres of our control." He turned for the first time to face his servant and put both of his arms on each of the round man's soft shoulders. "Do you know what we must do, Tofting?"

He shook his head wildly from left to right many times, excited.

"We must love one another. We must raise our families together. We must instruct our wives and our children to intermingle. We must come to truly KNOW one another Tofting. I must teach you and yes, you, you must teach me also, dear Tofting."

Tofting's knees began to rattle. It was not any colder than it had been before, in fact the sky had now grown lighter, but the idea the King spoke of was so strange to him it made him tremble. Amidst all the strangeness of his proposition however, only one question seemed to float up from his simple mind to mouth. "What'll our children do, lord?"

The slightest hint of a smile came over the previously grave and sullen face of the King. "Perhaps yours shall dance and mine shall sing!"

Tofting smiled. "I like dancing, lord. My lady does too."

"Then perhaps you will teach me."

"Gladly lord. I would gladly teach!" A smile comes over Tofting's enlivened face. The smile lasts five thousand years.

They mount their horses and continue on. The sun has just risen from behind the mountain and warms their backs. The warmth lasts five thousand years.

Peregrine! Flower's Flying!

The textual butterfly fills air with a portion of peregrine

Why use any other word?
It flutters!

The fulsome butterfly *kinds* and
Cuts up the slices of feeling
From inside a human eye which on-looks

If a child saw one for the very first time
I would say,
"The flower's flying!"

A Gradual Grasp for Paradise

Where we will flock t'ward, in
Pinion rushes of
Friendship enthuse

Slum child

      Run child

           Go live a little lie in the wide old sky

Where we congregate above the high noon air
Tweeting and silencing and meeting and kissing

At the very front
A well-intentioned, quiet and inconspicuous
Starling speaks English with an Arabic accent

      –Tone of brown-gentle–

He weaves upon us a very simple instruction to which we do not object:

"Please stand shoulder to shoulder, brothers
Keep a straight line."

And the wishes of pigeon and eagle alike are
Sewn into one cohesive kernel

A calendar of prayer

Canticle of our carbon aspiration and

Cairo of our slum

We chant cholla bread twists of rounded nuance
While we wait for wisdom bodies to be born as pregnant
Within us

And as we know, tails will follow heads.

Here I go

Shade is constantly moving
Moving on me

And when my eyes are raw
And when I close them
I always see a bird
Flying in the sky

And it's so profound

And then a fart shows up (or leaves?)
Making a quiet, but still ridiculously absurd noise
Curling upwards

And I am human again.

Only a human can live with such incongruities
Such mess
Inconsistency

Mediocrity and profundity
I wish they didn't link arms so often
Link arms and dance together.

I didn't know either of them had a sense of humour,
And yet they both wear a sick smile as they dance
Knowing I'm watching and trying to make sense.

Who would have thought?

Thought and Fart?

Crazy zeal. Zany creases in life.

Put your purpose in the box

And give it a good shake.

                                          Open the box

And look inside

If it hasn't disappeared entirely
You can bet your arse it's not what it once was!

A feeling I felt whilst holding a large, expensive and Beautiful Chocolate Cake in my arms

Oh, cakes!

Yes, I know, I know: I use far too many exclamation marks. But what else can I do? There is no other grammar. No other symbol! To express this FEELING!

The only replacement I can think of is an image of a monkey, sitting in the middle of a clearing in a vast forest at midnight. In front of him is an abnormally large, old, hardback book, propped up by a magnificently carved stand. The book golden-glows from its open pages and harkens back to the golden-ages. The pages are blank, but the monkey feels an inexplicable excitement, and so, without any knowledge of punctuation marks, grammar or even Roget's Thesaurus, he shoves his left hand out behind him, poos into it, then, bringing the hand around in one sweeping revolution, slaps the poo down onto the open page as hard as he can, making rabid chimp-exhortations and jumping up and down wildly.

AH(!)
AH(!)
AAH(!)

March of the Paki

"I wonder," says the judge before sentencing me,
"If there is a hell for paki's like you."

"Yes there is," I quip, full of beans and balls,
"ANTARCTICA!"

I say it like an 18th century American salesman
Pushing my right fist from right to left with a dip

"Antarctica it is then!" He says
Hammering his hammer to the hole that receives the
Hammer blows

I was sent off there in shackles and chains
And given a television with an inbuilt video recorder

I was given two videos:
Robocop
Which I would not watch because it was too violent, and
Irreversible
Which I also refused to watch because it featured some
Great sexual violence! ('*Two thumbs up!!!*')

"Smashing," I said
"I shall just have to find myself some other entertainment,
shan't I?"

I looked around and saw, as I always saw, a blank landscape
filled with snow and few variables.

I saw this in England and in America too. But at least there were no scared or hesitant people here. Such people bother me to no end. I had the guts to go out and commit crimes; what did they have the guts to do? Extract some useless nutrients then excrete the rest! And that's if they were lucky! If they weren't lucky they ended up with blonde hair and huge plastic, useless breasts, sitting around bored, in luminous pink boob-tubes, cooped up in a miserable house all the Summer long, whilst big brother watches them snore and fart with night vision. And pick their noses in the kitchen.

No, I'm better off here. And when Penguin Season is in, at least I'll have some good company.

Yes, some company!

A man needs company or else he'll go insane.
Yes. Totally Mad.

First Taste of Chocolate Salty Oat Cookie

Choom!
Challum!
CHAMPION OF WINTER!

You outlast it. That's how you beat it!
You mustn't be mature, no!
Oh no, my friend!
Mustn't outgrow your seasonal affective disorder!
Mustn't!
You must keep on believing that Winter is bad
And Spring, the redeemer!
Don't get too clever, it will ruin you.

Be a slow roller
An age guilder
A *kind of* winner
The vibrant sinner
It's a parrot inna mirror
A boulder in a river
A heart in a beginner
A start in the winter.

It's a myrrh-vellous moonshine
A Jesuit night-time
A Jesus chamber
A Managed manger

The Jesuit jungle is mechanical humble

And everything's lost on women who
Stare at other men when they're out with their boyfriends.

"Will you be my girlfriend?"

Will you befriend me? NOW?

Will you come into my moment?

But
Only if you promise
Disappointment!

Which, believe me, sister of humanity
You will.

Oh, ... YOU WILL

MWUAHAHAHA!
MOOWA-HA-HAR!
MOOWAH-HAH-HARR!

MOO!

<u>Poor Narrow Theory Babies!</u>

Static singular tunnels all leading circular lives of repetition are satisfied with themselves for no other reason than: they move with precision and empirical logic.

My time clock runs on a different magic

My face turns the other way today

So, deliver my head unto the doors of ever-inquisitive aesthetics lecturers and let them study it on their lunch break, after they have torn out and rent asunder the words of perfect poets.

So run, run, run in a circle!

Bilingual Butterfly

The bilingual butterfly knows exactly what you mean!

Don't even try and continue talking! No, really! Because what's coming out of your mouth is a mess anyway. It's not refined at all, and it backstab-betrays your truest feelings. He and she with the ears will not appreciate it, they'll take you for an enemy when in truth you are their closest. They'll get the wrong end of the stick; and what could be worse than the wrong end of the stick? They'll get the broom-dust in their eyes.

Trust that the bilingual butterfly bats his wings for you; wings which sing; wings dipped in beautiful scholarships and libraries; wings puffed on by soaring professor-heads.

All you must do is hold the others hand, in the middle of your verbal stumblage, and tell them that you don't know what you're talking about. They'll forgive and forget and flap their heads to the next topic. The next topic will eventually open itself up for you.

Be patient.

A sleeping ocean on a hot day.

No Such a Thing!

I shake my head in shambles!

There's no such thing as a particle!
I say to the clock at 3:36 am

No such a thing!

And don't get me started on fingernails and/or Psychology!

There aren't any!

Listen, Monkeyon…

"UH-UH! That's what I'm uh-uh… Trying… To do![4]*"*

And listen good, I'll say it very clearly

We are spirits. Not animals.

---

[4] Thundercats, series 01, episode 01

To Sufferers
For Herman Hesse, may God be pleased with him

Rotunda!!!!!!

Rest assured buddy
You won't be pickin' up cigarette butts off the pavement forever
You won't be lickin' your fingers in Kentucky Fried much longer

Stuck in grease-clouds.

The bastard-queue will soon be over

There IS a way back to the pleasures of youth
You're damn right there is!
Just sit tight there in the God-Rocket of rolling revivals!

...

If this were a modern Daniel Ladinsky-style translation of Hafez or some other trendy rendition of Rumi, it may be apt at this point to say something like, 'Take off your seat-belt!' or, 'Relax!'

BUT I WON'T!
Think I don't know what it's like?
Think I haven't felt it too?

When the heart gets farted on and whisked away to no-mans land by fate or by a faux-lovers controlling hand? When someone bites out a bloody chunk of you and spits it into the running-away river with no mercy as though it were a grenade pin? And your part-of-heart is white-water-fallen off and away to no-mans land?

I KNOW! In fact, let's be honest
I'm going through it right now!

So when I tell you to sit tight
That you're in the God-Rocket
I don't expect a finger snapping sea change
Or a wide grin of sudden inner peace!
NO!
I'm a pragmatist! Despite all the butterflies I see,
I'm a realist, dammit
I know there's no chance of an instant turnaround
An immediate ecstasy

More to the point
I know you don't want that
I know you don't want to be
Flip-switched to happiness just yet
And I know you're scared
And that me telling you that you're on a God-Rocket is
Rococo-madness
I know that whatever I say
You'll strap yourself in tight,
Clutch at the chair
Nails dug in
Tense
Your thighs

Your arse
Nervous
(The rides unknowable destination)

If it helps you for me not to call it a God-Rocket
Not to say that *things are unfolding as they should*
Not to allude to ripples in a pond
Or the unseen force which moves your body and mind
Every step of the guided, gilded, gallant way

Then I won't.

Just promise me you won't kill yourself yet.

In fact, don't worry, you don't even need to promise.

We both know you're going to make it.

Wage Slave

This is no way to spend the future
Unmended and medicated
Routine'd into silence
With no Coltrane running through the heart

This is no way to dive into tomorrow
Hesitant and filled with fear
Hanging on for dear life
To the secure bullet

.I must be let loose.

Somebody must make the zoo wild again
Let the rain fall in the living room

And my many children must appear in their multitude
Strung out as a laughing pearl necklace between my two
Accordion palms

Still In the World

Nothing died in me

I

Spermed a whale shot of ocean into the sky before
No eyes

Made the neighborhood pregnant with culture-change by acting strangely in public and allowing for silent observers to take mental note

Jumped into bed late on a Winters night - facedown to sheets - dancing and rushing with insane laughter as though the mattress were a newborn wife

Held my own hand in the dark and whispered beautiful thoughts to the black partickles which smiled and laughed but wouldn't admit it

And in day, as it is in life
I push the pushchair persistently
Even though the boy sitting inside it is also me
An overgrown boy

Cloudgazing and Cherrypicking
Persevering and shoulder aching

For Lawrence 'Ytzakh' Braithewaite, for Ishaq

Pile it on!

Keeeeeeeep it comin' now!
Left right Left right!
MONDAY TUESDAY WEDNESDAY THURSDAY FRIDAY SATURDAY SUNDAY!

PASS ME THE SPOON!

Tradition! <u>Living tradition</u>!

Where do we go though
When we get subtle and humble and quiet and have time to waste on imaginings?

Which curling crease in the cotton trouser leg
Do we run up?
Slime and wriggle up?
Shadow and silently
Faceless and thoughtfully

Such questions present themselves to you when
Once the mirror has responded with a gormless shrug
You are forced to turn away
And ask yourself inwards
With palms facing you and
Nose-vision on both sides,
"So... What am I, then?"

You are a random day off in the Winter
A bunking off from school afternoon
Sitting in a midnight highway
Lying down with a backwards moon on your
Upwards cheeks
Like a teardrop
                  Below your eyes
Or a mouthful

Fruit that nobody knows about
Somewhere underground, in a
Cypriot treasure-cave.

      You are a dead friend hung
      Who nobody knew
      Who died in a vacuum where nobody grew
      And sadness should be stifling
      But really it's just stunted

      And sadness should be stifling
      But really it's just shooed
      Away for today and the next day too
      Wait for the feeling to catch up to you.

      When it does it will satisfy
      Black day= good (for it pacify)
      Make full sense,   so no analyse
      Stone true life, still   paralyzed

But the subtlelight haze haz

Wholes in it
Size of white dustdots in window sunlines
Separated possibilities
Panicles of perfect dreams

.Ready to rain true.

Dreamscoops of half-moons like
Curling ice cream

Flirting upwards and slowly singing:
"Maybeee!"

You never know!

If (The merchant of tenderness)
For Prince Rogers Nelson

If I could, I'd try to sell Mandarin newspapers on the Beaches of Yemen

If I could, I'd ride elephants slowly through the beastly shopping malls of Houston, Texas
Seated on a piece of white canvas which drapes down its side and reads, 'believe'

If I could, I would marry you right here and now, live a full lifetime with you, smooth over every single rough edge and deliver you to absolute happiness

If I could I would fill all the huge modern glass buildings with sea-water and tropical fish and slow, smiling whales

I'd turn right forever and make funny faces at all the children I meet along the way

I'd make pockets in ties and heaters in shoes
I'd make rockets in eyes and whirlpools in you

If I could, I'd die right now and go straight to heaven

Der Lebenskünstler

Concern yourself with creating
  Collect things and set them free

Co-operate with everybody

Subjugate your self & remain silent!

Know nothing.
Expect nothing.

Keep on falling down
                        Black caves
 Alone
        And with loves

Have no standards
Remove your judgments
Shed your morals

They will still be there for you when you need them

Concern yourself with crying
Capturing
           Air
Of all colours and flavours
With your loose net of heartellect

Accept that you're a fake.

And don't be too pleased with the fact that you're
So wonderful.

Get in between your dreams and your
Days

And listen to the strange things your body
Says

The Poem of Delicious Affirmation

Don't crack up!

Realise this, wavering star cluster:

That there are shades of moon
Waxing away in a cave that holds
Deep inside your perfect ear

That there's semen and eggs freely socialising inside the
Womb of opportunity

Flirting with the chance to make hopeful
Irrational promises

Bursting with the desire to spurt out
Warm and hot utterances like,

I love you as much as nothing I know yet!

and

fuck this life! fuck it hard!

Where do we dance to?

We are on a wooden dance floor
Giant chess-board
Floating in space with the
Stars all around us

We dance like white people in films
Properly and dutifully
Your hand is on my sturdy young shoulder and
Mine is on your warm woman's waist

We're at the very edge of it
With eternity, dreams and destiny
Below and beside us

You bite your bottom lip and look up at me
Like a good girl contemplating a naughty act

But you needn't look that way
For my mind is also on jumping

I feel the same way you feel.

A Feeling, the weight of a Butterfly

Perceval. Palleme. Proser.
Point-in-fact. .Past.Time.

Where does it go?

If I wear a mink coat or a suit.
If I shave my head or let it go Lennon.
If I love and be loved or
                          Leave everyone
Laid out where they stand

What does it change?

Only your heart is sacred to me, my dearest
And no longer to rush you, wish I
No longer to encase and embrace you

Just to stand opposite where we behold each other;
Feel each others
Trembling presence

Continuing into one another

With no worldly wheeling
With no watchfulness
No wattage nor
Wasting of time, which is
Without time, in this, our
Wantless wish

And I Want to Break Free

And it was a horrible life I had lived. We were all underground. And it was dark. And there were puddles. The still black puddles of night. And there was a good hearted and kind woman, who had black hair and red lips; laying, strewn sideways across the cold floor in an evening dress. Neon lights and nightclub entrances reflected in the puddles around her. I was her abuser. I ran backwards and forwards every few moments, shouting horrible things to her, the worst of evils, the most vicious, seeping-in-words. Words that would never heal, that would linger like war crimes. And there she lay, mumbling to herself, unable to move somehow. All of the potential beauty that I had once sensed in her, when we first met, was now creased and folded and congealed. Dried tears and no energy left in her. We were all underground.

And then, everything changed. We were a population, or rather, representative of a population. Hundreds of us. Westerners. All dressed accordingly. A cross-section of a Western society. Workers. Slightly more English than American. And there, underground in a tube station, a sudden feeling of powerful immediacy swept across us. For me it was a feeling of rush, of sweat. I can't tell what it was for the others, all the other normal people, the commuters, women and men, suited up and living normal lives. But I had been living a bad life. A caged life. I had been going in circles of viciousness, constantly being hurt and then hurting and always ending up alone. So this sudden disaster-like feeling, this rush which descended upon all of us, from a silent power, was most welcome to me. It was escapism. A huge disaster is great news for city-lowlifes. We were being swept up and out of that place all together in a chaotic unison. Like scattering rats being shooed by the hand of a local caretaker God, or like excited little girls chasing after mid-60's Beatles. One or the other. We didn't seem to know whether or not to be happy or scared. Some smiled as they dashed, some squinted and tensed. We clamoured past one another, squeezing up the all-too-narrow London-like steps and bursting in our hundreds up barely functioning escalators, all striving for our own position, getting random cold hands in our faces and shoes on our shoulders, all grabbing and twisting and improvising and rushing.

And when we reached the top, the outside, the street, we were suddenly in New York City. It was spacious and tall, like downtown Manhattan, and also quite ornate and old-fashioned like the Upper West Side. It was beautiful and local, but it was a city, with blocks and uptowns and downtowns, all seemingly empty. The roads where the cars normally were, were not roads. From the pavement-Island around the exit of the underground, we all looked out and quite apart from the fact of there being no cars, the roads were not even made of concrete. The whole road was made up of an escalator-like girded metal, which had previously been moving in the most interesting ways. It was a cross between a tilted baggage-reclaim belt and an Airport moving sidewalk. It could move so very dynamically that you wondered what kind of technology made it possible. You wondered where you were. It had been moving like a surfers wave, and was so very fluid and capable. But now it was still.

And as the streets were empty, we all shuffled forwards, somewhat cautiously, but with smiles on our faces as we looked up at the soft blue light coming from the sky, in a pack, as commuters do, to stand on this strange metal surface. And when we did, when we stood in the middle of the place where cars would normally have been, we could look all the way down to the next block. It was close enough to make out a group of very well organized people, standing in straight lines. A marching band of sorts. But not quite like us, not quite with our concerns. Distant and regimented. Strange angels. They were not as important; it was their leader who mattered much more. He turned around to face us for a moment, with a twinkle in his eye, before turning back to the band. He wore a tuxedo, had dark hair. He was timeless. I turned to one of the ladies near me, slightly behind, and asked, "Is it Terry Wogan?" She looked back at me for a moment, but she was elsewhere, she was staring, on tip-toes and moving her neck trying to get a glimpse, with keen interest and a curious half-smile on her face, which despite being adult and attractive, seemed like that of a child. The leaders face did not really exist; rather, he seemed to be the physical embodiment of charisma, of enticement; a sort of host, or tv presenter for *existence*; absolutely in control of his every confident move and word. He had in front of him a microphone which hung upside down from a wire, the likes of which you will see at the start of a boxing match. When you followed the wire all the way up, you could see that it came from the clouds. The soft, warm blue clouds. Yes it was an overcast day, but warm and pleasant. The clouds were lower than normal, we felt as if we were locked in, but locked in somewhere good. The buzzing of the leaders voice through the microphone was so active and yet, one could not make out a single word of what he said, even though one was hearing it and it seemed to be in a language we could all understand. He seemed to be saying lots of clichéd things like, 'Ladies and Gentlemen' and talking about the 'Great show'. But he said none of those things explicitly. All one heard was a buzzing sort of sound, lightly distorted, like the voice that says, "Full steam ahead," and then makes funny noises in the song 'Yellow Submarine'.

And in a moment of happiness, I realized what all of this was leading up to. It was all for me. The others would get their time, when it was to be all about them (that was the whole purpose of this) but for that very moment, I thought of nothing but the excitement at my own predicament. I was overcome by the moment. The man had said the last thing he would say, as it turned out he was introducing something. And there it came, the music, in clarity, as if from gentle speakers booming down from across the sky, emanating as conjoined sound from every single particle around me:

Queen – I Want to Break Free

And so I parted ways with the group of commuters. I moved through the crowd as if I were being called, which I was, and I turned right into a smaller local street, so that I was leaving both the commuters and the band and their leader. As the music played and I sang along, I began jumping. And I could jump high! I could stay in the air much longer than normal and I could come down as slowly as I wanted to. I controlled the force by which my body came back down to the ground.

At one point, as I was floating on my way down, I moved to turn right in the air, which I did, and then I moved to turn left, which I also did, and just before I touched down, in rhythm with the snare drum, I kicked off the side of an ornate old building with all my strength and swooshed away to the right, landing at my own pleasure and walking again for a few steps, only to jump and fly again. I could not stop jumping. Because it felt so good, I was addicted to it.

And each time I leaped as high as I could into the air, with all my thigh-strength, first crouching down and then stretching out, arms up and ribs wide, lungs open and head shooting upwards, with wind on it, and always, each time, to and with the rhythm of the wonderful song; always feeling like the embodiment of those soaring synths, which kept on going and playing their moment. And each time, my chest felt so light and… Yes, and so free.

The author with a beautiful cake
Virginia, USA

Also available & coming soon from Yusuf Misdaq

Lefke Automatic / Destiny of Love (Poetry)	NEFI-BK07
The Beautiful / Palace Prayers (Poetry)	NEFI-BK06
Spilling Kingdoms (Poetry)	NEFI-BK05
Into Solidity (Poetry)	NEFI-BK03
Brighton Streets (Poetry)	NEFI-BK02
Pieces of a Paki (Novel)	NEFI-BK01
[No Title] (Documentary)	NEFI-CD03
Maghreb, Isha & Space (LP)	NEFI-CD03
Flowers & Trees (LP)	NEFI-CD02
From a Western Box (LP)	NEFI-CD01

Narayan (Novel)
The Steep Ascent (Novel)

www.ingramcontent.com/pod-product-compliance
Lightning Source LLC
Chambersburg PA
CBHW022123040426
42450CB00006B/818